LAND of
ALOHA

Cheryl Chee Tsutsumi
photographs by
Veronica Carmona
Ann Cecil
Ron Dahlquist
Philip Rosenberg

An Island Treasures Book

Island Heritage
PUBLISHING

LAND of ALOHA

THE HAWAIIAN ISLANDS

*H*ere's how
the birds view
Kāne'ohe Bay and
the magnificent
Ko'olau Range
on O'ahu.

Published and distributed by
ISLAND HERITAGE PUBLISHING

ISBN 0-89610-388-9

Address orders and correspondence to:

ISLAND HERITAGE
PUBLISHING
94-411 Kō'aki Street
Waipahu, Hawai'i 96797
Telephone 800-468-2800
        808-564-8800
Fax 808-564-8877
www.islandheritage.com

Printed in Hong Kong
First edition, second printing, 2002

PROJECT MANAGER: VIRGINIA WAGEMAN
DESIGNED BY JIM WAGEMAN

Contents

Welcome

TO HAWAI‘I

Hawai‘i. That single word evokes a montage of mesmerizing images. Verdant mountain ranges with serrated ridges rising more than 4,000 feet from the sea. Forests filled with extraordinary scents and sounds and textures. Groves of coconut palms nudged by breezes as warm and gentle as a kiss. Sunsets the color of gold and rubies, and a vast ocean that mirrors the dazzling sapphire of the sky.

The islands of Hawai‘i inspire pleasure, romance, and great adventures. Robert Louis Stevenson, Mark Twain, and Herman Melville chronicled their visits in captivating stories that remain classics in American literature. In 1873 the intrepid British author Isabella L. Bird spent six months exploring Hawai‘i on horseback, foot, and by steamship. *Six Months in the Sandwich Islands*, the book that resulted from her remarkable journey, is full of wondrous descriptions that in many cases still hold true.

LEFT:

*L*ook westward from Big Beach in Mākena on Maui and you'll see the uninhabited island of Kaho‘olawe anchored on the horizon.

FACING PAGE:

*V*isitors stroll along Kaua‘i's lovely Hā‘ena Beach, which is excellent for swimming and snorkeling during the calm summer season.

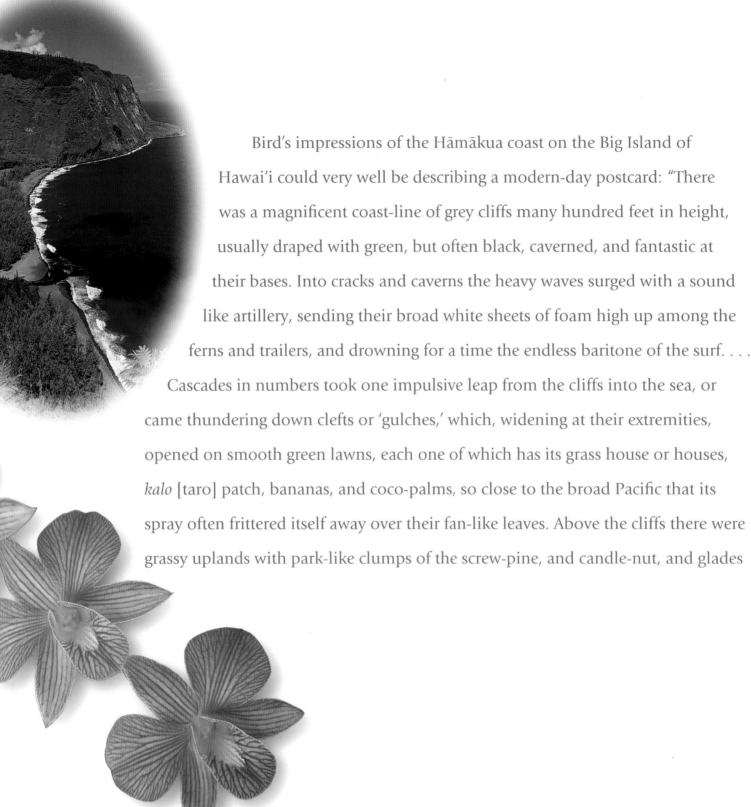

Bird's impressions of the Hāmākua coast on the Big Island of Hawai'i could very well be describing a modern-day postcard: "There was a magnificent coast-line of grey cliffs many hundred feet in height, usually draped with green, but often black, caverned, and fantastic at their bases. Into cracks and caverns the heavy waves surged with a sound like artillery, sending their broad white sheets of foam high up among the ferns and trailers, and drowning for a time the endless baritone of the surf. . . . Cascades in numbers took one impulsive leap from the cliffs into the sea, or came thundering down clefts or 'gulches,' which, widening at their extremities, opened on smooth green lawns, each one of which has its grass house or houses, *kalo* [taro] patch, bananas, and coco-palms, so close to the broad Pacific that its spray often frittered itself away over their fan-like leaves. Above the cliffs there were grassy uplands with park-like clumps of the screw-pine, and candle-nut, and glades

White-capped surf and a black sand beach fringe the entrance to Waipi'o Valley on the Big Island's Hāmākua coast.

FACING PAGE: Fragrant *kāhili* ginger adorns the Hāmākua Ditch Trail in Waipi'o Valley.

and dells of dazzling green. . . . Creation surely cannot exhibit a more brilliant green than that which clothes windward Hawaii with perpetual spring."

Separated by thousands of miles of open sea in every direction, the lush Hawaiian Islands, America's fiftieth state, are the most remote bodies of land in the world. Each year they lure nearly 7 million vacationers who initially come seeking a good time but inevitably leave with much more. A visit to Hawai'i is all about making connections with your heart, mind, and soul; discovering the miracle of life and appreciating its gifts—like sunshine and moonlight, birdsong in the morning, a perfect flower blooming along a secluded forest trail.

The beauty of O'ahu, Maui, the Big Island, and Kaua'i—their natural treasures, legends, history, arts, people, and architecture— shines on the following pages. Come, experience the magic.

Oʻahu

THE GATHERING PLACE

The deeply furrowed Koʻolau Mountain Range forms the backbone of the eastern and northern sectors of Oʻahu.

Diamond Head surveys a perfect day in Waikīkī.

Long ago a giant moʻo *(lizard) brought* pipi, *an oyster from far-off Kahiki (Tahiti), to the great harbor called Puʻuloa. There the succulent delicacy multiplied, for it could not be harvested during periods of* kapu *(taboo). In ancient times, the wise elders and* aliʻi *(royalty) strictly enforced the* kapu *during these seasons, so that fish and shellfish could thrive and thus provide food for everyone in the nearby villages.*

One day an old woman was wading along the reef of Puʻuloa, gathering seaweed. She put her hand in one spot in the coral wall and felt the small, hard shell of a prized pipi. *It was* kapu *time for* pipi, *but the woman looked around and didn't see anyone nearby. "I crave them, and who would know if I took a few?" she thought. She plucked a handful of oysters from the reef and placed them in her basket beneath a nest of seaweed.*

When she made her way back to the beach, she saw the konohiki, *the overseer of her district, standing there. "What have you been doing, old woman?" he asked.*

Aside from *pipi*, the oysters from which Pearl Harbor got its name, modern-day travelers will find just about everything else on Oʻahu. Its nickname is "the Gathering Place," and indeed it is—for culture, for entertainment, for education, for dining, for shopping, for business, for history. A cosmopolitan population of more than 870,000 (73 percent of the state's population) resides on this 608-square-mile swatch of the tropics, which boasts an intriguing blend of sophistication and down-home charm, high energy and laid-backness.

Much of Oʻahu's incredible past is shared through its attractions. In 1795 Kamehameha the Great's quest to wrest control of the island from King Kalanikupule ended at the soaring cliffs of Nuʻuanu. In what proved to be the final, decisive battle, Kamehameha's warriors drove the forces of Kalanikupule

"I have spent a few hours this morning picking seaweed," she replied, showing him her basket.

"Let me see," he said, taking the basket from her and closely inspecting its contents. "What have we here? Pipi? You have broken the kapu!" Angrily, he tossed the oysters and all the seaweed into the ocean and destroyed the basket. "You have disregarded the sacred kapu and may not take anything with you. Now go!"

The old woman was remorseful. She had indeed broken the kapu and deserved to go home empty-handed. But that was not enough. The mean-spirited konohiki followed her and demanded money from her, saying she needed to be further punished.

"Wasn't losing my seaweed and basket enough?" she implored. "Please reconsider. I am poor and have only one coin." But the greedy konohiki insisted, wanting the coin for himself.

The mighty mo'o saw everything that had transpired and was furious that the old woman had been punished unjustly. The mo'o collected all the pipi she could find at Pu'uloa and took them back to Kahiki. That is why although pearl oysters inspired Pu'uloa's English name, Pearl Harbor, very few can be found there today.

Named for a Hawaiian princess, Bishop Museum boasts the world's finest collection of natural and historical artifacts from Hawai'i and the Pacific.

Completed in 1882 at a cost of $360,000, 'Iolani Palace was the first building in Honolulu to be equipped with electricity. It also beat the White House and Buckingham Palace in this regard!

to the top of the valley and over the edge of the steep precipice onto the jagged rocks below. Few stories in Hawaiian history are as dramatic as this—or the view of windward O'ahu that's revealed at the 2,000-foot-high Nu'uanu Pali lookout.

The world-renowned Bishop Museum was established in 1889 by Charles Reed Bishop in honor of his wife, Princess Bernice Pauahi Bishop, great-granddaughter of Kamehameha the Great and the last direct descendant of the Kamehameha line. Feather helmets and capes that once belonged to royalty, handsome koa wood calabashes, and ancient Hawaiian weapons and hula implements occupy a particularly esteemed place in the museum's collection of priceless treasures.

In February 1845 Kamehameha III moved the seat of government from Lahaina, Maui, to the port of Honolulu on O'ahu, which was rapidly establishing itself as the center of commerce in the kingdom. In

Downtown Honolulu's skyscrapers dwarf ten-story Aloha Tower (off center, near the bow of the ocean liner), which was the tallest building in the city when it was dedicated in 1926.

Over 14,000 coral blocks quarried from offshore reefs were used to construct stately Kawaiaha'o Church.

subsequent decades, while Hawai'i's form of government changed from absolute monarchy to constitutional monarchy to annexation by the United States to U.S. territory to U.S. state, Honolulu never relinquished its role as the Islands' political, economic, and cultural hub.

With its imposing skyscrapers, endless streams of traffic, and packs of well-dressed executives, the core of downtown Honolulu mirrors any modern metropolis. But just a few blocks away, the past beckons: visitors can stroll through 'Iolani Palace, the residence of King Kalākaua and Queen Lili'uokalani, Hawai'i's last two reigning monarchs; the Mission Houses Museum, headquarters of the first contingent of Christian missionaries in Hawai'i; Kawaiaha'o Church, which has offered Sunday services in the Hawaiian language since 1842; and exotic Chinatown, with its open-air fish and produce markets, acupuncture clinics, herb shops, noodle factories, dim sum parlors, and Buddhist and Taoist temples, where smoldering joss sticks emit mesmerizing swirls of incense-laden smoke before dignified golden images.

Honolulu exudes an engaging vivacity. There's something exciting, something entertaining, going on all the time in this dynamic, cosmopolitan city—carnivals, craft fairs, luaus, parades, sports events, concerts, ethnic festivals, plays, dance performances, and more. In short, Hawai'i's capital offers every diversion imaginable.

Packed within the sophisticated seaside resort of Waikīkī, which measures just one half mile wide and two miles long, are award-winning hotels, elegant shops, first-class restaurants, and revues that rival the best Las Vegas has to offer in terms of drama and glitz. Waikīkī's smooth, cream-colored beaches—Hawai'i's most famous ribbons of sand—are the perfect places to dally and daydream. Standing guard over it all is landmark Diamond Head, so called for the calcite crystals that nineteenth-century sailors found sparkling on its slopes and mistook for diamonds.

end of the war—the USS *Arizona*, which sank in the 1941 bombing and now rests beneath a stately white memorial that revenues from Elvis Presley's 1961 Honolulu concert helped to build, and the USS *Missouri*, where the treaty ending World War II was signed on September 2, 1945.

Beyond Honolulu, O'ahu is miraculously transformed. Within sixty minutes of the city skyline, you can snorkel within the horseshoe-shaped rim of an eroded volcanic crater; cruise in a glider plane kept aloft by brisk trades; surf the most famous waves in the world; kayak to islets with curious names like Chinaman's Hat and Goat Island; and hike into secluded rain forests where only birdsong stirs the stillness.

These are just a few vignettes of a destination that enchants even those who've lived there all their lives. At once rustic and refined, serene and spirited, O'ahu is the island where people love to gather.

*T*he *Arizona* Memorial commemorates the beginning of World War II. It marks the spot where the battleship USS *Arizona* sank when Japanese warplanes bombed Pearl Harbor on December 7, 1941.

*O*ver 35,000 men and women who fought in World War II and the Korean and Vietnam wars have been laid to rest in the National Memorial Cemetery of the Pacific (Punchbowl).

On the outskirts of Greater Honolulu, Pearl Harbor remains the focal point of an important chapter in American history. On Sunday morning, December 7, 1941, Japanese warplanes roared over the harbor, dropping bombs on the U.S. Navy's mighty Pacific fleet, which lay peacefully at anchor. That attack propelled America into World War II, which was to drag on for nearly four more long years.

Today Pearl Harbor is home to the two battleships that have come to symbolize the beginning and the

*A*loha Tower is the centerpiece of a bustling shopping, dining, and entertainment center.

FACING PAGE, CLOCKWISE FROM TOP LEFT:

*I*olani Barracks housed the Royal Household Guards; Hawai'i's governor lives in Washington Place, the former home of Queen Lili'uokalani; a statue of Lili'uokalani is near the State Capitol; a plaque at Washington Place commemorates Lili'uokalani and her most famous musical composition, "Aloha 'Oe"; Mission Houses Museum showcases early missionary life.

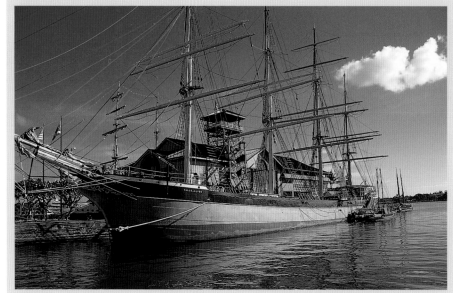

CLOCKWISE FROM TOP LEFT: *B*ishop Museum's Hawaiian Hall; *Falls of Clyde,* the only fully rigged, four-masted ship afloat; courtyard at the Honolulu Academy of Arts with sculpture by Jacques Lipchitz; Queen Emma and King Kamehameha IV enjoyed vacationing at this Nu'uanu retreat, now known as Queen Emma Summer Palace. RIGHT: *H*awai'i Convention Center offers state-of-the-art facilities, including 200,000 square feet of exhibition space, nearly 150,000 square feet of meeting space, and a 36,000-square-foot ballroom.

*W*aikīkī's glittering
skyline lightens
the somber mood
of night.

*H*ula dancers perform seaside at the Sheraton Waikīkī.

*T*his statue on Waikīkī Beach honors famed beachboy Duke Kahanamoku, who won gold medals in swimming at the 1912 and 1920 Olympics.

*O*pened in 1927, the elegant Royal Hawaiian has been nicknamed "the Pink Palace."

*B*lessed with a beautiful beach, shallow waters, and abundant marine life, Hanauma Bay is a wonderful choice for swimming, snorkeling, and people watching.

RIGHT:

*M*akapu'u Point, O'ahu's easternmost landmark, over-looks Makapu'u Beach, Hawai'i's most famous bodysurfing spot.

LEFT:

*W*aimānalo Beach
skirts the base
of the verdant
Ko'olau Mountains.

*F*loating off
Makapu'u Beach,
67-acre Mānana
islet, popularly
known as Rabbit
Island, is protected
as a sanctuary
for seabirds.

A full moon
rises over the
Mokulua islets.

*R*inged by the
regal Koʻolaus,
Kāneʻohe Bay is
a lovely setting
for water activities
of all kinds.

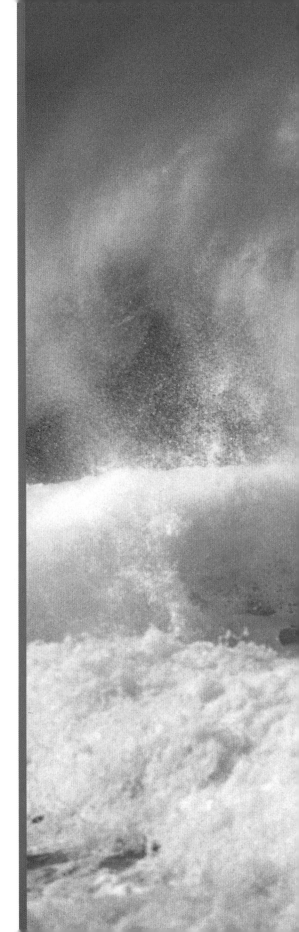

*T*he best wave riders in the world converge at Sunset Beach every year, hoping to win big money in big-name surfing competitions.

*H*ale'iwa highlights on O'ahu's North Shore: surfboards galore, eye-catching signs, trendy cafés and shops, refreshing shave ice, and pareus in a vivid palette of colors.

*D*esolate Ka'ena
Point lies at the
westernmost tip
of O'ahu.

*B*lue skies crown
Wai'anae Valley.

Maui

THE VALLEY ISLAND

With clear, calm waters that deepen gradually, Wailea Beach is a wonderful choice for swimmers.

Exploding in a brilliant burst of light at the summit of Haleakalā, sunrise signals the start of a new day.

One day when Māui the demigod was fishing with his three brothers off Kaupō, on the east side of the island of Maui, he noticed a big fire burning on the mountainside. How could this be? The Hawaiian people had been without fire for a long time. They had saved glowing coals when the great volcano Haleakalā erupted but had been unable to keep them alive. Thus their diet consisted of raw fish, fresh fruits, and uncooked roots and vegetables. They longed to learn the secret of making fire so they could once again savor hot, cooked food.

Māui and his brothers paddled to shore as quickly as they could so they could pinpoint the source of the fire. As soon as the canoe hit the beach, Māui leaped out and raced up the mountain—but he was too late. All he saw was a group of mud hens stomping out the last embers, and they flew away as soon as they saw him.

Like its legendary namesake, the island of Maui leaves a lasting impression. "Maui nō ka ʻoi," residents like to say. "Maui is the best." It's hard to argue with that; the Valley Island is indeed bewitching.

When seen from the air, it resembles a human head, neck, and torso. The island is actually two dormant volcanoes—Puʻu Kukui (the "head") to the west and Haleakalā (the "torso") to the east—joined by a low, flat isthmus (the "neck"). Scientists say these immense land masses were born as separate seamounts on the floor of the Pacific Ocean. Underwater eruptions continued for countless millennia, and the submarine mountains grew bigger and bigger, taller and taller, until they finally emerged above the undulating waves. Subsequent

For days afterward Māui and his brothers quietly followed the mud hens, hoping they could learn the secret of fire making, but the crafty birds, knowing they had unseen, unwanted company, did not oblige. Finally, Māui proposed that he stay behind while the other three went fishing, but the mud hens counted the men in the boat and knew one was hidden, watching them. Only when they saw that all four brothers were out at sea in the canoe did they make fire.

Māui wasn't about to let the birds outwit him. He rolled kapa (tapa) in a thick bundle and propped it up in the canoe so it looked like a man. While his brothers launched the canoe, he concealed himself behind trees where the mud hens gathered.

Meanwhile, the birds counted the figures in the boat and assumed all the brothers had gone fishing. Good, they thought. It was safe to make fire. But before they could do anything, the impatient Māui jumped out from his hiding place and grabbed the oldest bird by the neck, threatening to kill her if she did not tell him the secret of fire making.

Even with the demigod's strong hands wrapped around her neck, the bird was reluctant to reveal the truth. She first told him to rub the stalks of water plants together. When Māui did this, only water dripped out from the twisted stems.

lava flows eventually fused the two volcanoes into one 729-acre tropical paradise.

Three-quarters of Maui's land area is uninhabited wilderness, including Haleakalā National Park, which stretches some 28,000 acres from the barren summit of the volcano, down its southeastern slope to the verdant Kipahulu coast. Haleakalā National Park is Maui's biggest playground. Three thousand feet deep, with a circumference of twenty-one miles, the volcano's enormous crater could contain the entire island of Manhattan, skyscrapers and all. Active travelers can indulge in camping, hiking, biking, and horseback riding in a spectacular setting that resembles the face of the moon.

Local people call the fertile belt that wraps around the midriff of Haleakalā Crater "Upcountry." Here, at a cool 3,000 to 4,000 feet above sea level, farmers tend flourishing fields of carnations, roses, proteas, cabbages, and onions so sweet you can eat them raw.

Angrily, Māui held and shook the mud hen harder, until she said, "Try rubbing reeds together!" But no fire flared up from the slender, delicate stalks, which easily bent and broke in the demigod's firm grip. Furious, Māui further tightened his hold on the mud hen's neck until she cried out, "You must use green sticks!"

Māui chose two young, green sticks and rubbed them together vigorously, but not a single spark appeared. He had now lost all patience with the defiant mud hen. He squeezed and wrung her neck until she was half dead and finally relented. "The secret of fire making," she gasped, "is in dry wood."

At last, when the demigod rubbed two dry sticks together, they ignited. "There is now only one thing left to do," he said. He took another dry stick and ran it over the top of his captive's head until her feathers fell off and only bare skin remained. And that is the story of how the Hawaiian people learned how to make fire and why to this day all mud hens have bald heads.

In 1802 Kamehameha the Great named Lahaina the capital of the Hawaiian kingdom, and so it remained until 1850 when Kamehameha III moved the government seat to Honolulu. The lusty port also won distinction as the center of the whaling industry in the mid-nineteenth century, with a record four hundred ships calling in 1846. There never was a dull day in town, as irreverent sailors clashed head-on with puritanical New England missionaries. Herman Melville, one of the young whalers who visited Lahaina, immortalized the colorful era in his epic novel *Moby Dick*, published in 1851.

Lahaina still displays a lively spirit. Nestled among wonderful boutiques, restaurants, and art galleries are vivid reminders of its colorful past, including an authentic replica of a nineteenth-century brig, a wooden prison dating back to 1852, and a museum that was the residence of one of Hawai'i's most revered missionaries. In short, Lahaina is a great place to wander.

The majority of Maui's population is concentrated in the central part of the island. Here, too, are its

county seat (Wailuku), its major harbor and airport, and the bulk of its businesses. The last remaining acres of sugarcane on Maui are planted on this isthmus, as is the island's first notable arts facility—the Maui Arts and Cultural Center.

Central Maui packs a lot of punch. At its southernmost point, Māʻalaea Harbor provides a picturesque backdrop for the Maui Ocean Center, the largest tropical aquarium in the United States. Among its sixty-plus exhibits is a 750,000-gallon saltwater tank that visitors walk through to enjoy a marvelous 240-degree view of sharks, manta rays, various fish, and other intriguing marine life found in Hawaiian waters.

Meticulously fashioned from scrubland, the luxurious resorts of Wailea in south Maui and Kāʻanapali and Kapalua in west Maui host more than 2 million visitors each year. Their swank properties boast state-of-the-art spas, valuable collections of artwork, award-winning restaurants, and magnificent landscaping—all designed to appeal to the most discriminating of travelers.

In striking contrast, the east coast hamlet of Hāna is tranquil, uncrowded, and cloaked in a thousand shades of green. It is a place where the people are as gentle as the breezes, and the beauty of the land is more astounding than anything man has created of concrete, steel, and glass. Hāna soothes. Hāna calms. Hāna heals. It has provided the perfect retreat for those escaping the hubbub of everyday life, including celebrities such as Carol Burnett, James Garner, Richard Pryor, George Harrison, Jim Nabors, and Kris Kristofferson.

Pristine forests and valleys, precious history, posh hotels—it's rare that a place can be all things to all people, but that precisely is the magic of Maui.

Imaginative minds could dream up many explanations for ʻĪao Needle's intriguing shape, but the real story is quite simple. Eons of rain and wind eroded the exterior layers of a stone formation, leaving the basaltic spire we see today.

Ulua Beach is one of five cream-colored crescents that adorn the resort area of Wailea.

Seen from Kapalua, Moloka'i is framed by white clouds, bright pink bougainvillea, and the deep blue of the Pailolo Channel.

If the arms of Honolua Bay could be extended, they would touch the eastern shore of neighboring Moloka'i.

The Baldwin Home Museum in Lahaina provides a valuable glimpse of nineteenth-century missionary life.

Crumbling walls are all that remain of a fort that was built at the height of the whaling era to monitor the ships that packed Lahaina Harbor.

Opened in 1901, Pioneer Inn, with its distinctive red roof, offers commanding views of the harbor and streets of Lahaina.

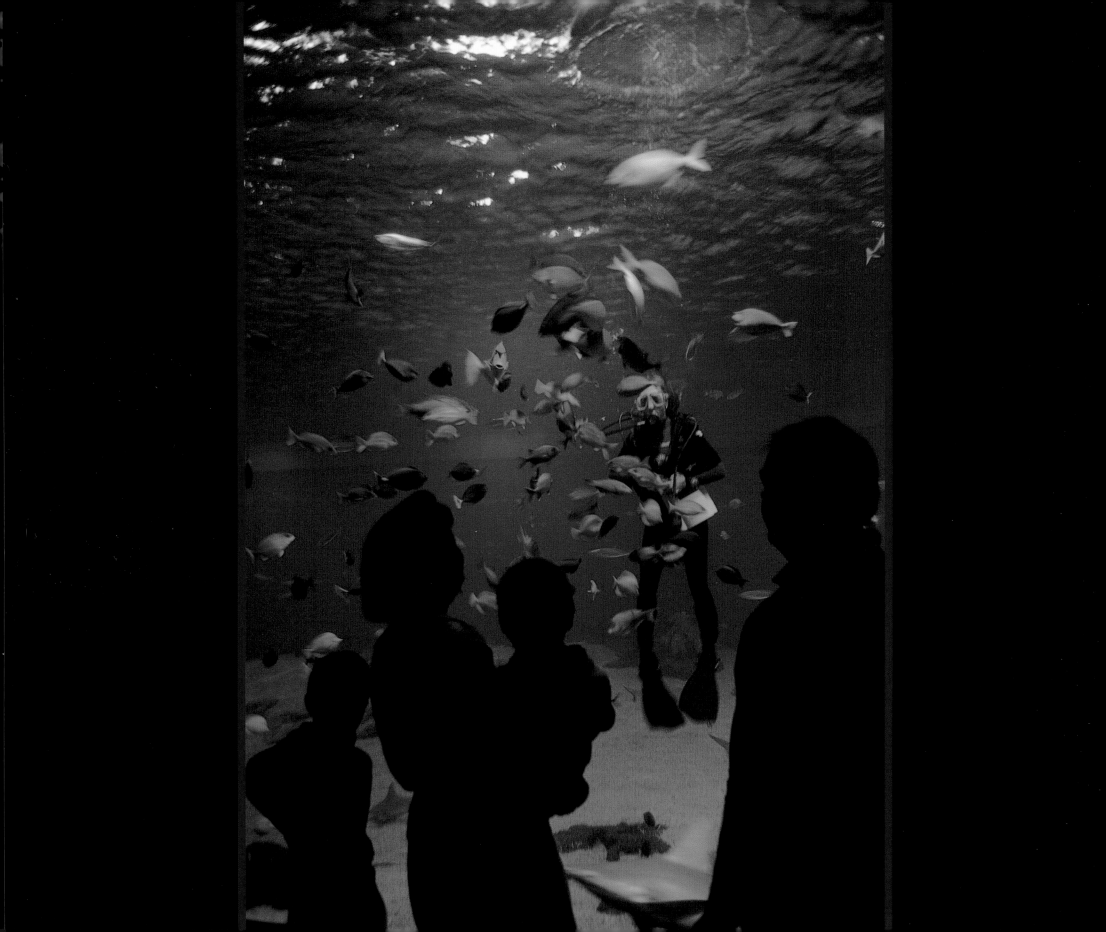

*L*andlubbers can learn all about the sea at the Maui Ocean Center (facing page and right), which features more than sixty exhibits, including a 750,000-gallon saltwater tank that's home to nearly two thousand fish, sharks, turtles, stingrays, and other fascinating creatures.

*T*he Maui Arts and Cultural Center in Kahului is the island's premier venue for presentations of the performing and visual arts.

*O*ld storefronts harking back to the turn of the century give Pā'ia a nostalgic appeal.

*M*onstrous swells at Ho'okipa Beach provide adrenaline-pumping challenges for intrepid wave riders.

FACING PAGE:
*T*he sunny resort area of Wailea wraps around some of the best beaches in Hawai'i.

*I*n Mākena, a 360-foot cinder cone named Pu'u Ōla'i separates Oneloa or Big Beach (right) and

Little Beach, also named Pu'u Ōla'i. Cinder cones are hills formed by the accumulation of volcanic debris.

*J*ust outside of Makawao, Hui No'eau Visual Arts Center offers art classes, demonstrations, exhibitions, and a noteworthy gift shop. Originally the home of prominent Maui residents Harry and Ethel Baldwin, the Mediterranean-style villa was built in 1917.

*L*ooking like a set from "Bonanza," Makawao fits perfectly into Upcountry's rustic lifestyle.

With the world's largest dormant volcano as its centerpiece, Haleakalā National Park sprawls over 28,655 geologically diverse acres. Haleakalā Volcano's massive crater—an otherworldly montage of cinder cones, lava flows, and mini craters—is 7 ½ miles long, 2 ½ miles wide, 3,000 feet deep, and 21 miles in circumference.

The silversword can be found on Maui only above the 6,000-foot level of Haleakalā.

*T*he road to Hāna presents a spectrum of fabulous views, including this one of Honomanū Bay.

*S*ilvery waterfalls often pierce the deep green raiment of the Hāna Highway.

*O*ne of Hāna's best beaches, Hāmoa is a popular playground for experienced swimmers, surfers, and bodysurfers.

The black
sand beach at
Wai'ānapanapa
complements
the rich green of
the landscape.

Lovely Hāna
Bay basks in the
glow of sunrise.

Hawai'i

THE BIG ISLAND

Two girls sat roasting chunks of breadfruit in the upland plains of Ka'ū. "They look as though they are done," said the older girl. "I am famished! I'm sure they are ready."

Sunset embraces Pu'uhonua o Hōnaunau, an ancient place of refuge on the Kona coast.

Sparks fly and the earth glows; few sights can match the awesome beauty of Pele's pyrotechnics.

As she poked the steaming breadfruit with a stick, the younger girl noticed an elderly woman walking below them along the trail. "Look at that old woman! She has a walking stick and she's limping. I should go help her climb up this hill."

"Why bother?" replied her friend. "She's just a stranger, not family. And anyway, the breadfruit is cooked. Let's take them out of the coals and cool them."

As the girls were pushing aside the coals and pulling out the breadfruit, they heard a voice. "Please may I have some food? I'm so hungry. I have put nothing in my stomach all day." Startled, they looked up and saw the frail old woman standing close beside them, leaning against her walking stick.

"We have nothing to share," the older girl snapped. "There is only enough for ourselves and our families."

Sultry and demure, lush and austere, perky and subdued—just like the volcano goddess Pele, the island of Hawai'i, appropriately called the Big Island, presents an amazing range of moods and faces. It's as though the Almighty Creator wasn't quite sure what to do with its 4,038 square miles, so he blessed it with a bit of everything.

Within an hour or so you can go from sweltering desert to cool rain forest, from palm-fringed beach to snow-capped peak. In fact, geographically speaking, the Big Island is the most diverse in the Hawaiian chain, boasting eleven of the thirteen official climates known throughout the world (only arctic and extreme desert conditions aren't found here).

The seven other major Hawaiian islands could fit within its borders with plenty of room to spare, but

But the younger girl smiled and invited the woman to stay. "Sit on that rock over there, and I will bring you some breadfruit," she said. She put half a breadfruit on a large leaf and brought it to the old woman, who quickly ate it. The kind-hearted girl brought her another generous piece, and that, too, was gone in moments. The old woman then asked for water, and the girl offered her gourd to her guest, saying, "Drink as much as you like."

When the old woman was finished, she stood up and said to the younger girl, "Your elders have taught you well. Go home and tell your parents to hang strips of kapa *(tapa) at the corners of their house for ten days. That way, they shall be kept safe."*

As soon as her mother and father heard the tale, they knew the stranger was Pele, the goddess of the volcano. They hung the strips of kapa *as Pele had directed, and when ten days had passed, liquid fire erupted from Moku'āweoweo, the summit crater of Mauna Loa. Down the slopes of the mountain came the molten lava, destroying everything in its path, including the home of the older girl's family.*

But before the river of red-hot lava reached the house where the younger girl and her family lived, it forked, flowing in streams on either side of their home and gardens. Pele had kept her promise and spared her young benefactor's loved ones and their property.

"big" only begins to describe its many wonders. Think superlatives. Barely 800,000 years old, the Big Island is the youngest island in the Hawaiian archipelago and was the first to be inhabited. It claims the southernmost point (Ka Lae) and the wettest city (Hilo, the county seat) in the United States. America's only commercially grown chocolate is produced in Kea'au, on the east side of the island, and the country's finest commercially grown gourmet coffee (priced at about $35 per precious pound) thrives in Kona, on the west side.

Measuring sixty miles long and thirty miles wide, and containing ten thousand cubic miles of solid rock, Mauna Loa is the largest mountain in the world. More than 90 percent of all the stars visible from Earth can be seen from atop neighboring Mauna Kea, where the W. M. Keck Observatory houses the world's largest optical/infrared telescopes.

Hawaiian history is peppered with tales about Kamehameha, the first in a long, proud line of monarchs

At Parker Ranch rodeos, the best cowpokes in the state exhibit their prowess at riding and roping. Lots of thrills and occasional spills are all part of the show.

Men, women, and children representing ancient *ali'i* (royalty) make their way to the beach at Pu'uhonua o Hōnaunau for a traditional purification ceremony.

who ruled Hawai'i for nearly a century. This great warrior king, who is credited with unifying all the islands under one rule, was born near 1,500-year-old Mo'okini Heiau in the North Kohala district around 1758.

Emerald pasture carpets Waimea, home of 225,000-acre Parker Ranch, one of the oldest and largest ranches in the country. The ranch was founded by John Palmer Parker, a sailor from Massachusetts who jumped ship on the Big Island in 1809. He subsequently befriended King Kamehameha I, married a Hawaiian princess, and in 1847 began amassing the verdant acreage now known as Parker Ranch. Hollywood couldn't have come up with a better script.

Kohala's most imposing landmark is Pu'ukoholā Heiau, the last major ancient Hawaiian place of worship built in the Islands. Other archaeological gems —including petroglyph fields, cave shelters, house sites, fishing shrines, ancient footpaths, and fish-

ponds where mullet was raised for the enjoyment of the *ali'i* (royalty)—are woven in a necklace of resorts along the sunny coastline of South Kohala. Posh oases in an otherwise desolate lava landscape, these resorts rank among the finest in the world.

Most visitors recognize Kona for its superb fishing and robust coffee. The district's most valuable asset, however, still goes largely unnoticed; unbeknownst to many, it harbors one of the richest troves of archaeological treasures in the Hawaiian archipelago. Within its boundaries can be found the remnants of ancient villages and battlegrounds, grassy slopes for riding *hōlua* (sleds), lava-tube burial caves, fishponds, *pu'uhonua* (places of refuge), petroglyphs, *kū'ula* (stone fishing shrines), and *heiau* (places of worship).

History maintains a powerful presence in Kona. Kauikeaouli, Kamehameha III, was born near Keauhou Bay, and it was at neighboring Kealakekua Bay that Captain James Cook met his demise. Other histori-

cal landmarks include Moku'aikaua Church, the oldest Christian church in Hawai'i; Hulihe'e Palace, a favorite summer retreat of King Kalākaua; and Ahu'ena Heiau, where Kamehameha I meditated and conferred with his advisers and *kāhuna* (priests).

Pele, the volatile volcano goddess, definitely has left her mark in the Volcano region, a geologic wonderland of ebony *'a'ā* (rough) and *pāhoehoe* (smooth) lava fields, gaping calderas, and searing steam vents that can melt the flesh off a fish in seconds. Amazingly, also found here are *kīpuka* (lush pockets of plants and wildlife miraculously spared by raging lava flows) and verdant rain forests where *hāpu'u* ferns and *'ōh'ia* trees grow so densely they block out the sun.

A powerful energy pervades Volcano—a special spirit the Hawaiians

call *mana*. As in a church, you enter the area with reverence and awe. You instinctively know that this compelling place must be sacred.

Hawai'i Volcanoes National Park, the state's number one attraction, sprawls over 377 square miles of the Volcano district, encompassing a visitor center, hotel, restaurant, art center, museum, and observatory where volcanologists keep close tabs on seismic activity. These buildings appear insignificant, however, amid the drama of nature's beauty; from the tiniest, most delicate of flowers to craters as large as lakes, she reveals her many miracles here.

Immerse yourself in the spirit of this extraordinary place. You won't be disappointed. The Big Island of Hawai'i promises big surprises and even bigger rewards.

*N*ative to the Himalayas, the *kāhili* ginger, unlike other members of the large ginger family, grows well in cool areas such as Volcano. It gets its name from its resemblance to the *kāhili,* the feather standard that was symbolic of Hawaiian royalty.

*P*uffy clouds of steam rise as molten lava meets the sea in Hawai'i Volcanoes National Park.

A kama'āina (longtime resident) enjoys some sun and quiet time beside Hilo Bay. Snow-capped Mauna Kea rises in the background.

*H*ilo, America's other "city by the bay," wraps around picturesque Hilo Bay.

*T*his stunning view of the Waipi'o Valley shoreline can be seen from the Waimanu Valley Trail.

The centerpiece of a lush state park, 'Akaka Falls tumbles 442 feet into a foliage-lined pool.

In Waipi'o, *lo'i* (irrigated terraces) for growing taro are tended by a handful of farmers who relish the seclusion the valley offers. When Captain Cook arrived in Hawai'i in 1778, there were 4,000 people living in Waipi'o. Today the valley claims only about 50 residents.

*S*een from Mauna Kea, sunset paints the sky off Waiko-loa to the west with broad strokes of vivid color.

*C*louds hover along the western flank of Mauna Kea.

*A*s amazing as it may seem, snow blankets the summit of Mauna Kea every winter.

In 1790 Kame-
hameha I built
Pu'ukoholā Heiau
in honor of the
war god Kūkā-
'ilimoku on the
advice of a *kahuna*
(priest) who
told him he
would unify
the Hawaiian
Islands only after
he did so. This
war temple
has been desig-
nated a National
Historic Site.

Sunrise imbues
the Big Island's
northern coast
with a mystical
aura. Rugged and
remote, this mag-
nificent twelve-mile
area stretches
between Pololū
and Waipi'o valleys.

*K*amehameha I is said to have been born near 1,500-year-old Mo'okini Heiau, which was supposedly built in a single night by 18,000 men who formed a human chain and passed stones for the temple hand to hand from Pololū Valley, fourteen miles away. Hawaiians today still use the grounds for religious ceremonies.

*S*et beside the sea, Lapakahi State Historical Park harbors the remnants of a 600-year-old Hawaiian fishing village, now partially reconstructed.

*S*pecial events in Kohala—many of them centered around the area's *paniolo* (cowboy) heritage—bring out a rainbow of beautiful colors, costumes, and faces.

*T*his pastoral Parker Ranch scene could be right out of a Hollywood western.

FAR LEFT:

A lovely crescent
of soft white sand,
Kauna'oa Beach,
which fronts the
Mauna Kea Beach
Hotel, draws
dozens of sun
lovers every day.

*S*waying coconut
palms frame a fish-
pond in 'Anaeho'o-
malu. In olden
times, mullet, *moi*,
and other fish were
raised in ponds like
this solely for the
consumption of the
ali'i (royalty).

*D*edicated in 1837, Moku'aikaua Church in Kailua-Kona town is the oldest Christian church in Hawai'i. It was built from rough-hewn lava stone and mortar made from crushed and burned coral mixed with *kukui* nut oil.

*N*estled by the sea, lovely Hulihe'e Palace (marked by its green roof) is another Kailua-Kona landmark.

*L*ong ago Puʻuhonua o Hōnaunau was a sanctuary for defeated warriors and people who had broken the *kapu* (taboos). Today the 180-acre site is a national historical park preserving three *heiau* (temples), replicas of traditional *hale* (houses), petroglyphs, fishponds, a variety of native Hawaiian plants, and a massive stone wall measuring 1,000 feet long, 10 feet high, and 17 feet wide.

The volcano area's terrain includes steaming crevices and lush rain forest, as at the entrance to Thurston Lava Tube. Lava tubes form when flowing lava crusts over and the molten core eventually flows away.

A young girl admires an *ōhiʻa lehua* blossom, the official flower of the island of Hawaiʻi.

Rivers of flaming lava hardened into artistic formations when they cooled.

Kaua'i

THE GARDEN ISLAND

Spectacular views of the Nā Pali coastline unfold along the Kalalau Trail.

Sunlight and shadows dance on the ridges of Mount Wai'ale'ale.

Summer was the season for the gathering of feathers—the time when the bird catcher Maunakepa, his wife, Ho'olei'a, and their daughter, Helohelo, lived in the lush mountainous region that stretched from Kaunuohua to Mount Wai'ale'ale. All through these months Maunakepa would roam through the rain forests, setting traps for the 'apapane, olokele, 'amakihi, and 'ō'ō, whose feathers were prized for the capes, cloaks, and helmets worn by the ali'i (royalty).

As she grew up, Helohelo watched and learned. She was a healthy, pretty child, with rosy cheeks that had inspired her name. One day, however, Helohelo became very ill. Her worried parents knew they had to find a kahuna lapa'au, a healing priest, to cure her. Before the sun rose, Maunakepa was on his way to the nearest village to seek help.

On the way, he saw a man dressed in white, sitting in the shade of a tree. The man greeted him and asked why he was in such a hurry. When Maunakepa explained, the man said, "You're in luck! I am a

Think green. Think pristine valleys, magnificent canyons, and soaring peaks. Think taro patches, fragrant gardens, and wide open pastureland. Paint these pictures in your mind and you'll see vignettes of Kaua'i, the oldest of the major Hawaiian islands and arguably the most beautiful.

Born a little over 5 1/2 million years ago, the Garden Island is, in fact, a 549-square-mile garden in perpetual bloom. At its heart is wet and wild Mount Wai'ale'ale, which is refreshed by rainfall nearly every day of the year. Wai'ale'ale is the centerpiece of a stunning mosaic of meadows, valleys, rain forests, and sheer, furrowed cliffs that defines Kaua'i.

Up north, adventure begins where the paved road

kahuna lapaʻau. But you must give me and Lonopūhā, the god of healing, shrimp and ʻawa (kava, a narcotic drink) in exchange for the medicine that will make your daughter well."

Maunakepa agreed. It was late afternoon when he finally returned to the priest with the shrimp and ʻawa. In return, the priest gave him a small gourd containing a liquid that he said would cure Helohelo.

But the medicine did not help; if anything, it seemed to make Helohelo's fever worse. Although Maunakepa and Hoʻoleiʻa prayed through the night and never strayed from their daughter's sleeping mat, she died in their arms in the wee hours of the morning.

In fact, the man who had called himself a kahuna lapaʻau *was no priest at all. He traveled from village to village claiming he could treat the sick. He collected generous payments in the form of food and clothing, then disappeared before people discovered the charade.*

Seeing this, the great god Lonopūhā came to the land where mortals lived to rectify the situation. He found the charlatan sitting beneath a koa tree, eating the shrimp and drinking the ʻawa that Maunakepa had

ends at Kēʻē Beach. This is the gateway to Kauaʻi's famed Nā Pali Coast—twenty-two awe-inspiring miles of fluted cliffs, some soaring 3,000 feet above the undulating Pacific. Four pristine valleys—Kalalau, Honopū, Awaʻawapuhi, and Nuʻalolo—are tucked within the bosom of these cliffs. All of the valleys are uninhabited and accessible only by foot, boat, or helicopter.

The northern town of Hanalei is fringed with taro patches and cute to the point of being quaint. Despite its down-home demeanor, Hanalei reveals flashes of sophistication in boutiques where you'll find handblown glass vases, trendy tropical apparel, one-of-a-kind jewelry, and other fabulous buys.

Boasting splendid views of Hanalei Bay, Princeville is 11,000 acres of carefully planned opulence. The exclusive resort community encompasses a luxury hotel, single family homes, condominiums, townhouses—and all the amenities that go with them,

brought him. Looking into his heart, Lonopūhā saw he carried no remorse for his deceit, and in a fit of anger, the god turned him to stone.

Traveling to the mountains, Lonopūhā found Maunakepa and Ho'olei'a sorrowfully burying Helohelo. Although he could not bring their daughter back to life, the god appeared to the grieving parents in a dream and told them to closely watch the grave.

One day, Maunakepa and Ho'olei'a noticed that a small shoot had popped up from the grave. The shoot grew into a bush no one had ever seen before. It bore berries that mirrored the rosy color of Helohelo's cheeks.

When the high chief of the district heard about the strange new shrub, he came to see it for himself. No one could tell him what the plant was or where it came from, so he prayed to Lonopūhā. Answering his prayers, the god told him, "This plant is the color of Helohelo's rosy cheeks. It shall be named 'ōhelo in honor of her."

The high chief declared the 'ōhelo bush and its fruit kapu, forbidden to everyone. As time passed, birds spread the berries throughout the mountains and forests of the island. The 'ōhelo still flourishes there today, among the other natural treasures of verdant Kaua'i.

Motorized barges transport visitors two miles up the Wailua River to the Fern Grotto, a popular wedding site.

including two golf courses, a tennis club, spa and fitness center, shops, stables, and trendy restaurants.

Nature has strewn her wonders in the Wailua region of east Kaua'i, including the Fern Grotto, a magnificent cavern that's draped with an abundance of hanging ferns, and Keāhua Arboretum, a lush haven pierced by an ancient trail that leads to Mount Wai'ale'ale. Centuries ago, the Hawaiians made annual pilgrimages up Wai'ale'ale to honor Kāne, the god of creation, sunlight, fresh water, and forests.

Considered very sacred in ancient times, this district also is known for its many *heiau*, including Holoholokū and its adjacent birthing stones. It was imperative that the offspring of Kaua'i's *ali'i* be born at these birthing stones or they would be stripped of their high rank. Likewise, if a commoner was able to give birth here, her child was endowed with the status of a chief.

South of Wailua is Līhu'e, Kaua'i's unpretentious county seat, which might go unnoticed save for such

*V*isitors explore Kaua'i's scenic southern shore on horseback.

*P*o'ipū claims its own Old Faithful—Spouting Horn, where energetic wave action forces seawater up through a lava tube as high as 50 feet in the air.

attractions as Grove Farm Homestead, once a flourishing sugar plantation; the Kaua'i Museum, with its fascinating exhibits of koa furniture, quilts, shells, weapons, tapa, and other Hawaiiana; and Kilohana, a stately Tudor-style manor built in 1935 by sugar magnate Gaylord Wilcox.

The sunny south shore reigns as Kaua'i's most popular visitor destination. Po'ipū Resort wears a lei of lovely beaches; within a mile-long stretch of picturesque coastline, water babies can indulge in a literal ocean of activities, including swimming, surfing, boogie-boarding, snorkeling, and diving. Recent diggings have yielded a trove of archaeological treasures in Po'ipū, including coral and sea urchin files, bone awls, fishhooks, round stones used in the game of *'ulu maika* (bowling), adzes very likely wielded by Hawaiian canoe builders, and other vestiges of fishing villages that dotted the area some 400 years ago.

In a word, western Kaua'i is extraordinary. The range in climate here is astounding—from warm and dry along the sun-splashed shore to cool and moist more than 4,000 feet above sea level in the verdant mountain regions. Forty-five miles of well-marked, well-maintained trails crisscross Kōke'e State Park, 4,345 acres of wilderness perfumed with native plants such as *maile, mokihana, 'ōhi'a lehua,* and *iliau*. Many endangered native Hawaiian plants and birds thrive in the ten-square-mile Alaka'i Swamp, which borders the east side of the park.

A fifteen-minute drive from Kōke'e, Waimea Canyon is a remarkable example of nature's handiwork. Mark Twain dubbed it the "Grand Canyon of the Pacific," and grand it is—3,600 feet deep, one mile wide, and ten miles long.

It's no secret that Hollywood loves beautiful Kaua'i. More than sixty movies and television shows have been filmed on the Garden Island since 1933, including *Raiders of the Lost Ark, Jurassic Park, South Pacific,* and *King Kong*. And now many travelers are discovering what Hollywood filmmakers have known for decades—Kaua'i is indeed a star.

FACING PAGE:

*T*he late afternoon sun sets the ocean and cliffs of Nā Pali afire.

*L*imahuli Stream flows through pristine Limahuli Garden in Hāʻena, which is part of the National Tropical Botanical Garden.

*T*he paved road ends near rock-strewn Kēʻē Beach at Hāʻena State Park; from this point on, Kauaʻi's north shore is all glorious wilderness.

FACING PAGE:

*A*ncient *kalo* (taro) terraces are still tended at Limahuli Garden, which was first settled by the Hawaiians about 1,500 years ago.

*C*oconut palms flourish on the hill above Kaulu Paoa, near Kē'ē Beach, a *heiau* that once served as a school for historians and genealogists. Nearby is Kaulu o Laka Heiau, dedicated to Laka, goddess of dance, where hula instruction once was given.

*H*analei Bay shows off a shoreline scalloped with cream-colored beaches.

*T*he town of Hanalei retains the rural feel of Kaua'i's north shore.

PAGES 108–9:
*A*bundant rainfall makes Hanalei Valley an ideal location to grow taro. The corm of the taro plant is cooked and pounded with water to make poi, a staple in ancient Hawai'i.

These scattered
rocks in Lydgate
State Park near the
mouth of the
Wailua River are
the remnants of
Hikina a ka Lā
Heiau. This place
of worship was
built across the
river from Wailua
Nui a Hoʻāno,
where Kauaʻi's
kings once landed
their canoes.

Mullet are
raised in the
900-foot-long
ʻAlakoko Fishpond,
which legend
says was built by
the Menehune.

The twin cascades of Wailua Falls tumble 80 feet into a foliage-lined pool. Long ago, the *ali'i* (royalty) would dive from the top of the falls into the pool to prove their courage and prowess.

Graceful waterfalls add to the east side's allure, among them 'Ōpaeka'a Falls.

Each year, thousands of visitors admire the splendor of the Fern Grotto.

FACING PAGE:

*W*aves crash against the rocky coastline of Keoneloa Bay in Poʻipū.

*O*ne-hundred-acre Allerton Garden in Lāwaʻi is part of the National Tropical Botanical Garden, which was chartered by Congress in 1964. One of Queen Emma's summer vacation homes originally stood on the site, and she planted the first seedlings for her garden there in the 1870s.

*W*aimea town's main street is bordered by modest shops and restaurants.

A montage of crags, buttes, and ridges, the "Grand Canyon of the Pacific" shows off breathtaking textures and colors that change with each movement of the sun and clouds.

PAGE 118:
*T*he myriad hues of sunset swirl around Kalalau Valley.

PAGE 119:
A couple plays in the waters off Polihale Beach, one of the widest and longest beaches in Hawai'i.

References

Bird, Isabella L. *Six Months in the Sandwich Islands.* Honolulu: University of Hawai'i Press, 1964.

Mrantz, Maxine. *The Hawaiian Monarchy: The Romantic Years.* Honolulu: Tongg Publishing, 1974.

Pūku'i, Mary Kawena, comp. *Folktales of Hawai'i.* Honolulu: Bishop Museum Press, 1955.

————. *Hawai'i Island Legends.* Honolulu: Kamehameha Schools Press, 1996.

————. *The Water of Kāne and Other Legends of the Hawaiian Islands.* Honolulu: Kamehameha Schools Press, 1994.

Westervelt, William D. *Myths and Legends of Hawai'i.* Honolulu: Mutual Publishing, 1987.

Wichman, Frederick B. *More Kaua'i Tales.* Honolulu: Bamboo Ridge Press, 1997.

Williams, Julie Stewart. *Kamehameha the Great.* Honolulu: Kamehameha Schools Press, 1993.